THE BORGO OF
THE HOLY GHOST

May Swenson
Poetry Award Series

THE BORGO OF THE HOLY GHOST

poems
by

Stephen McLeod

UTAH STATE UNIVERSITY PRESS
Logan, Utah

Utah State University Press
Logan, Utah 84322-7800

Manufactured in the United States of America.

"The Dead" was first published in Slate Magazine, www.slate.com. Reprinted with permission. Slate is a trademark of the Microsoft Corporation.

Grateful acknowledgment is made to the editors of the following publications where versions of these poems first appeared:
Agni: "Broken Gull"
American Poetry Review: "What Comes Through Hearing"
Barrow Street: "All Roads Lead to Kansas"; "Donation"; "The Shoulder Where It Belongs"; "That Crazy Moon"
Bay Windows: "Just the Facts"
Columbia: A Journal of Literature and Art: "Chronic"; "The Goldberg Variations"
The Journal: "Late Reading"; "My Brother's Ghost"
The Paris Review: "At the West Street Piers"; "The Borgo of the Holy Ghost"; "Just By Deciding It"
Ploughshares: "Becoming Kansas"
Shenandoah: "Pieta" (appeared originally as "Michelangelo's Pieta")
Slate: "The Dead"
Southwest Review: "A.D."
Western Humanities Review: "Against Stevens"; "An Exercise For Lovers"; "For Barbara & Vincent"; "Heaven Reassigned"; "Speaking in Tongues"; "What to Do What to Say".

Some of the poems in this book are dedicated as follows:
"Donation" is for Peter Covino
"The Borgo of the Holy Ghost" is for Joe McLafferty
"Creation" is for Michael Cuomo
"Just By Deciding It" is to the memory of Brent Pierce
"All Roads Lead to Kansas" is to the memory of Dean Yates
"What to Do What to Say" is for Richard Smith, Jr.

Special thanks to my parents, and to Peter Boyle, Lucie Brock-Broido, Mark Harden, Scott Hightower, Richard Howard, Barbara Holton, Jack Myers, and Vincent McKenna.

Library of Congress Cataloging-in-Publication Data

McLeod, Stephen, 1957-
    The Borgo of the Holy Ghost / Stephen McLeod.
        p. cm. — (May Swenson Poetry Award series)
    ISBN 0-87421-421-1 (alk. paper) — ISBN 0-87421-420-3 (pbk. : alk. paper) — ISBN 0-87421-422-X (e-book)
    I. Title. II. Series.
    PS3613.C58 B6 2001
    811'.6—dc21
                                                                2001001474

for José Joaquin Zuleta Colon

CONTENTS

ONE

TWO

THREE

FOREWORD
A Note on Stephen McLeod's
The Borgo of the Holy Ghost

SO ASSURED IS THE UTTERANCE HERE, SO CONVINCED THE DICTION AND
so swift the procession of tropes, that I suspect the most availing strat-
egy for a new reader (it would be a literalism to call Mr. McLeod a
"new" poet, for he incessantly reverts to practiced stanzas, sonnets and
sestinas, a litany of old contraptions and even older disciplines, of which
more presently)—for a *new reader*, then, beset by so many discoveries all
at once, so rich a designation of wonders, best to adopt this drastic
approach: *in the destructive element immerse*, that is, read right through all
the poems as if they were one apostolic statement, a continuous and
continuously deprecated handling of what can never be grasped, only
beheld. As his ironic title reminds us, this poet's burden is transfigura-
tion—ever aspired to, evidently withheld, eventually bestowed...

Then, after such commitment to the whole body of McLeod's poetry,
it will be easy—it will be easier—to "figure out" (surely the right formu-
lation here) the individual limbs and organs, separate citations of loss
and recovery—"loss" being a name for the life lived, "recovery" for the
poems achieved. On those rare and remarkable occasions such as this
one when the poet we newly come to is all of a piece (though such a
piece be given in fragments, in erasures, in dilapidation and collapse), it
is all too common to be flummoxed by the singularities of performance,
by the separate (and, say, unpunctuated) address:

Every human wants to say something always to each thing in the road
Before it is a road or the tire tracks that are not specifically sayings but

The witnesses of the sayings that even the grocer's daughter keeps
As lazy and natural as a dollop saying each day like a baby each thing

Rare and secretly awful the ordinary sayings the things changed
By being said into the one saying them the one creating them

Separating them into the things they are and will be and new things...

And besides McLeod's individual poems, each with what I might call
its chaotic cosmos to confront, there are all those overriding allusions to
the great dead, the Makers (for all his range of afflatus, McLeod is a

worldly poet—he believes other people exist), chosen painters and sculptors so rhapsodically evoked—how did Rothko, Rodin, Joan Mitchell and Pollock gain their apotheosis, along with heroic monsters such as John Brown and Nietzsche, the horns and hoofs of historical record? If we new readers are to assimilate so much hardware, we had better do it by moving right along, reading with the momentum of persistence, at least for the first time around.

"Around" it is, or will be: the poet's method, his practice, his *usage* is one of inveterate recurrence: first movement or thesis, aspiration to a perfected experience of being; second movement or antithesis, failure, the inevitable collapse of such hopes, what Hegel calls the scandal of the negative; third movement, the synthesis, which is, in religious terms, sacrifice (making-holy). I spoke earlier of the older disciplines which are McLeod's unfailing resource. Readers will recognize the ancient ceremonies of initiation which are at the root of all poetry, the myth or mouth of sacred utterance. Once the *askesis*, the stripping-away has occurred, the helpless acknowledgement of dearth and deficiency, then (only then) transfiguration may be reckoned and the words of rapture granted:

> Our bodies embark their seasons steady as weather.
> Crosswinds meet on the ridges and crowd the air.
> The sky is a glass of water. We are that good.

I am proud to salute Stephen McLeod as the fifth recipient of the May Swenson Poetry Award. He is a new poet after all, and a noble one, chastened by the time's disinheritance yet by his own numinous utterance a master of our shared experience as fallen men and women.

Richard Howard

A poet and translator, Richard Howard is Professor of Practice in the School of the Arts (Writing Division) at Columbia University in New York City.

THE BORGO OF THE HOLY GHOST

ONE

DONATION

I would make some small thing for you to hold in your hand.
It would be black, smooth, blue in the right light.

I would give this object to you secretly, slip it in your pocket.
You wouldn't notice its soft weight as it slid past the hip,

As it found its right place. I can still hear you
Waking me: it was a long drive, gone so long

I've forgotten who you are till you say my name,
Till I hear my name, sit up straight and think that you're Jesus.

What I would give you is the stone that fits the stone-hole perfectly,
Its contours conforming so clean that you would not notice, for a time,

That you never walked so balanced and tall, you never saw a street so rare,
Your own name a bell unbending the stooped man to his full solemnity.

A solid word I would give you to stop up the wind that pulls us all
Into itself till we are nothing but density. This would prevent you,

In all your days, from the frost at the window, from the narrow lake,
That then you would not be afraid as your body goes its long way over.

BECOMING KANSAS

My friend says *yes* to this, *yes* to that,
    Lies in bed all day saying answers,
His life reduced each hour to this: water,

        Paper-thin sheath of flesh, various cancers
That he allows, even befriends.
    Some of us will die of greedier

Diseases, some by our own skeletal hands.
    Others will flicker out; a few will rage.
My friend looks through his window to land

        Draped over itself in green velvet bulges:
Rippling fields, uninterrupted ocean
    From eye to horizon that pulses

With deepening shadow. He used to run
    In those fields. The corn was shoulder high.
Awaiting blindness, he says *yes* again.

    With body inside-out the door's his eye:
Turning to everything, everything enters him.
    So I infect him when he looks at me.

All night he coughs up blood and phlegm.
    The lungs want air, not scenery. Next day,
He sits up in bed and chooses hymns

    For his funeral. If he can stay
Still like this, his body's broken gates
    Unhinged, allowing everything to be

Inside him, saying *yes* to anything that wants
    A body to consume, he thinks
He can become whatever he loves.

    That is why he does not break,
And why the ceaseless answers, always the same.
    And even though tomorrow he will wake

and cough half an hour, expelling his dreams,
    He'll start again, and in fourteen days
He will finish this task. In death, the seam

    Of his body quietly separates,
The word his mouth surrounds now spoken best:
    Eternal, without pitch or beat,

The true music intended when I say *yes*.
    He sings this where we buried him as he
Lets in the winter through his melting breast,
    And Kansas, which he will become, and me.

THAT CRAZY MOON

I can't get enough of the moon. It's all over the place.
First it's there lounging above that warehouse
On Christopher Street, the one near the piers
Where everybody does absolutely
Everything. You can be sure of that.
Next day it's coy behind a blue tree,
Blue as ice in an ice commercial, tipped like a hat,
Thin as a grandmother's teacup of tears.

And of course it's the easiest love. Poems are lousy
With it. A man walked there, Sea of Tranquility,
It enthralls even more, the moon in June, our first blind date.
I went out once on a blind date that lasted, like a cotton rose.
There it was, big as a cow, orange, drowsy,
Wedged above one of those
Unimaginably expensive townhouses
Where some elderly diva I imagine

Relives every day of her life backwards. Dreams!
It rises for me still whenever I wait for it,
Glad as a fungo with nowhere to fall.
I watch on 10th Street an Attic portico
For some sign that not only can a blind date
Turn out for the best, hand in hand, nowhere to go,
Just schmoozing through the moonlit Mews,
The beginning of an entire lifetime, unexplainable,

But also that we stand amazingly upright,
Opposable thumbs, chiaroscuro blue,
Athena from a shellfish, poetry,
That the sky cherishes us, an enormous Other,
Not like anyone's Father, not quite like a mother.
It is morning now. It is twilight soon.
And there she is, and everything is true.
That's the moon for you. That crazy moon.

ANDANTE CON MOTO

1.

This stands for what I cannot say,
the stone I cut, the chaff I sweep away,
    the quotidian

task of bodies shedding the ore
to their natural center and last door,
    as far from the mind

as future, as a child's too trusting reach.
This is my only job, to cut and search.
    You lean in that same

doorway as though you could know from
tapped sounds the distance they travel to come
    to you, to arrive.

If I *could* say this I would say:
You are ever an absence to me, a
    music with no text,

a vocalise suspended in
a haze so gray I almost miss it when
    it swells into tongues.

This leaves me breathless. But it leaves
me nonetheless. Make no mistake: I love
    language and its works.

But I would change to hold *you* in my mouth
for the length of a lozenge. This is the truth.
    This is the whole truth.

2.

At *Hotel Oceana*, Garcia the Dog,
his mouth full of April flowers,
    is leaping and leaping.

From the balcony his lover,
impatient, stares at the sea. He never
    notices the street.

He believes this is a sign of
character, believes that in this way love
    will discover him.

But character is Tosca as
her hand drops the knife, as she remembers
    to outline the cross

on the forehead of a dead man
she killed just to see you once more, one
    dawn before the birds.

She knew it would end like this. She
needed it to end like this, having given
    herself so fully

to Art. Her back lifts the breast and
places exactly in reach and at hand
    one breath at the world's

last ridiculous parapet,
inevitable clash: *O Scarpia,*
    avanti a Dio!

    3.

I've wasted a good deal of my
life trying to tell you they are not lies;
    they are not dreams; there

are ways of ending that do not require
perfection, only balm. To be here
    is to do something

flawlessly. I refuse to dream
because no matter how bad it gets some-
    one loves me; this is

clear from the cellos that tell the
secrets of every created thing.
　　　I believe in this:

what is not here fashions me, proof
of our bodies, the glow of going loose.
　　　I am coming out-

doors now to walk in the snow, to
disturb it. I will walk such a long way
　　　at last to become

unremarkable. This is how it ends,
no augmented thunderclap, only this:
　　　two skies connected,

the charged space between them, how to
listen, what to say when the roan mane spoons
　　　your splendid shoulder,

and the music relaxes to
staggered rows, and the right words gather in
　　　short, still sentences.

THE SHOULDER WHERE IT BELONGS

*Why am I so determined to put the shoulder where it
belongs? Women have very round shoulders that push
forward slightly; this touches me and I say: "One must not
hide that!" Then someone tells you: "The shoulder is on the
back." I've never seen women with shoulders on their backs.*

Coco Chanel

A torch song *slightly touches me*
     but I try to ignore it because
       I am working before working

but what can I do   The radio has
     very round shoulders that push   forward slightly

        I'm thinking about
my mother's pearls in a high school picture
       you know it's not real it couldn't be
but   *Don't Explain*   she was always
    determined even then
to put the shoulder where it belongs

last week I took to the streets where it is whispered
     the Rasputin of Peru has men on every corner
they put your head in one place and your feet in another
    and no one will miss you   that is his secret

exquisitely the women wear their   *shoulders on their backs*
and they do not wake from these rendezvous
    he is that clever

O to be a victim
    gliding Fifth Avenue deviant aloof
     heads turning   whispering   nodding
in that knowing way

       I confirm
your deepest fears   one day you will wake up
       your shoulder where it doesn't belong

and I will be there next to you watching
    as the rose light exposes your shadows   your shoulders fabulous
        and backwards

OF BEING AND ESSENCE

Every human wants to say something always to each thing in the road
Before it is a road or the tire tracks that are not specifically sayings but

The witnesses of the sayings that even the grocer's daughter keeps
As lazy and natural as a dollop saying each day like a baby each thing

Rare and secretly awful the ordinary sayings the things changed
By being said into the one saying them the one creating them

Separating them into the things they are and will be and new things
How sometimes it is misty and the streets seem dangerous

But the danger is quiet or perhaps it is smothered there in neutral colors
Taking on ordinary sounds in the background no one actually listening

A small error in the beginning is a war in the middle and silence
And then no one is saying anything but staying still and amazed

As she has her adventures and goes along the road on her safety tires
Daydreaming or thinking about the kids how beautiful and odd

But she cannot exactly know that she is thinking this it is too
Beautiful and queer and exposed and wet and creaking in the sharp air

What she says is in her hands you can see the blue veins on the topside
On the other side you can see the white imprints of the stillborn words

The glossalalia of what she will be yet on a Sunday maybe
When the snow is still full and holy in the strange light

THE EXECUTION

What were you doing the day it happened?
How did you learn of it?
What did you do then?

Augustine

That day you were playing in the dirt. You rolled
Dirt cigarettes in newspaper. Hot or cold,
You never noticed. You learned of it slowly,
        The way bugs slow down

In the light or winter, the way a voice goes
South. So many days have become only *then*
Or *ago* or *when I was a kid*; details
        Lurk in blurred borders.

You want to break out. Always, in everything,
To step back into your shadow till the birds
Can see through you and the heat doesn't enter
        And nothing matters.

What did you do then? You started to die too.
You began without knowing. But dying, the
Participle, has no clear beginning till
        The moment it's said,

And already it's over, the one pure thing
The one did who did it, who was doing it
Without knowing, perfectly. Someone exhales
        And then it's finished,

As though a whole life of anticipated
Joy is one breath, one glimpse at the new light just
Clearing the horizon as the axe falls clean,
        Swift, with the careless

Surprise of that day you heard it whisper from
The periwinkles in your grandmother's dark beds,
In a flock of boys, and you kept quiet, and
        You knew it was true.

LOGO

When the last word is
spoken it will be
gasoline the left-
over groceries
roll idly nowhere
stop now forever

there within the light
of trees light shuts down
a city's ruined
vast canyons over
the red sky a last
banner fading some-

one's voice echoing
O the ripe days gone
the fiorellos
scattered like useless
money and no song
lingers no dust sounds

THE BORGO OF THE HOLY GHOST
(Rome: Christmas night, 1991)

The earthly city affords its shrug-of-shoulder luster
    simply by being there.
Not avarice or lust or even pride preserved it.
    I set my course toward
The simplest, pinkest light. And if I find myself
    in love, for example, or caught
By the slightly unsettling glare of someone's constant attention,
    it isn't the point of life.

At the end of the tunnel to our right, a waist-high marble plaque
    reports, by a straightish line
Engraved below the Latin, its cursive script difficult,
    the level the Tiber crested
In 1274. Above, a shrine of more
    recent vintage: an overturned
Glass of flowers singed by a votive light recently spent,
    itself knocked over.

The better guidebooks will miss, while noting the genre,
    such windows as these.
That same year (we could be told) Aquinas collapsed and found
    the long-awaited answer
To questions never asked at Lateran IV, where he
    forfeited his seat to Another.
And seven centuries later you are born while somewhere
    another flood threatens.

Remarking a disaster or even a rendezvous
    with battered almanacs
Can signify the sense that some things are important,
    especially when they're cut
In the best Italian marble. But everyone has a birthday,
    and this, at least, implies
That someone loves you enough to tell you what it is.
    We get by on our looks in the end,

[16]

By what we've weathered or by what we've allowed.
   I can't think of anything better
To hope for than the plowed and planted meadow where
   I've cast my seed with yours
And waited for a generous summer. And so I am led to you
   by ancient lanes and tunnels,
Routes long established for someone else's shortcuts,
   prayers and landmarks.

This plaque is not conceivably near today's *Lungotevere*. Still,
   I suppose it's the same river.
And as we emerge, my heart, unhinged, releases its rudder:
   Before me, unexpected,
Lit by cool fluorescence, the Pantheon appears like the Host
   Raised in a seamless monstrance.
Christmas night. The edge of a suddenly antique sky
   spills over, accommodating

The pillowy glow that rises from discreetly placed lighting.
   I touch with my whole hand
A large, bewildering column, pocked as the moon, and solid.
   I listen for the sound
Humming beneath my fingers of two thousand years.
   I have never touched anything
So unmistakable. Nothing stranger. *I forgot to tell you about this,*
   you say, inscrutable, smiling.

EASTER IN BELGRADE, 1999

Here the gathered hush
Joins the light dimly.
The only sound's the risk
Of sound before the sound
No one can hear until
Its echo crashes grimly
Into the battered fragments
Of explanation. Ground
Sustains it, though heavens trill
In developing segments.
And now the world is brisk
With nothing, and lush

With the unspeakable.
In lunar cities the halls
Are dark and shocked with noise
As brutal histories
Combine to wedge the age
To its millennial
Appointment. Sadly, the strains
Of Bruckner in the breeze
Prove illusory. Rumors
Of another monster's passage
Exaggerate even as the walls
Of Belgrade crack and stumble.

Exiled beauty seethes
From music to pronouncement.
Hawks cry from the cathedral
Where a bishop sourly swings
His Easter thurible.
A missile from heaven breathes
Its wondrous alleluia,
And Christendom, chest-high,
Repeats its yearly, inscrutable
But no less urgent announcement:
The Lord is risen indeed!
The blood of Abel sings.

A.D.

Newborn and starved for news, Theophilus
Receives the heft of Acts from the climate-cracked
South. The glad sun seems to wax.

                                       Elitist
But otherwise accurate Tacitus
Remarks, almost in passing,
The light's odd surge of brilliant noonday glamor
As, after the fire, while porcine Nero naps,
His scapegoats one by one collapse
In the garlanded arena. He sighs and hopes for the best.

Amidst all this unsightly clamor
Few seem to notice, as the old world flowers
Each springtime to its last,
That once unrivaled gods capitulate,
And gleaming towns are crushed beneath their weight,
And once again the days have left their hours
To gather at the edge of the faltering age
Wedging in V-formation toward its throat.

And fewer still will see
A light green carpet on the pale slopes grassing
The empire under, or the crowds that lie
Like hordes fast-frozen by some trick or art,
Who feed each other there by hand, by heart,
And spread to a glowing blur on the horizon.

AT JOHN BROWN'S GRAVE

I am feeling so empty this May after three years the same thing;
I need to go up, see the sights, take in a little of the last
Cold air before Life. So I come here. It isn't hard to find,
Just off the highway at one of those towns whose sole reason
For existence is a famous shack, a grave, a barn
And the tallest mountain in New York state.

I don't know, maybe I have a nervous condition, but I stand at
The fence getting sunburned and I'm thinking, *why?* A woman
Who lives just off the federal parking lot or whatever it is seems
So excited to see us like a happy Labrador. I watch her
Running from a hundred yards away, clutching her floppy ranger
Hat, slowing down to a trot, fanning herself—*Whooee!* she complains,

Cheerfully, cautiously. Who are these two, she wonders.
The thought passes; she's just so excited to give us the grand tour.
There are four or five buried, a son or two, a comrade, someone
Else I think. Just a bunch of nuts if you want to know. What's strange
Is that everyone *does* know this, the night in '57 he dragged men and
        boys from
Their beds and quietly split their skulls. Osawatomie John.

And there's a boulder like the one at Pollock's grave, who, incidentally, was
Recently featured on a postage stamp without a cigarette—there was much
Debate about the cigarette. And standing there I couldn't help thinking
        about Pollock,
The last person who should have occurred to me, except he too
Was possessed, driven, but that's pretty obvious so I stop thinking about
Pollock's brain sprays and his little barn outback, also preserved, and I

Remember that my friend and I drove hundreds of miles upstate
To lay eyes on this rough place and, of course, the famous
Mountain. It says something about me, I think, and about America
That this is an official place. That the tiny house he built, the failed
Farm, the stone-yard there, is watched over by the government
And a fan club. What kind of hero is this? What kind of father?

I think it was Strong who wrote, *He only told us what time it was.*
But I'm not sure. I scoured the diaries unsuccessfully one week in
April trying to find this, so maybe it was Douglass. Anyway,
I suppose that it's true, though it should be argued we didn't need *him*
To tell us that. He must have told something though. All those kids
And wives crammed into this three-room shack. All ready to die

For men they never knew or loved except in some abstract, harsh
Old Testament way. But when I think about everything I've read
To prepare myself, and even before, it seems this haunting
That spread like infection to stragglers and sons is what I am. Essentially.
Daguerreotypes show his character well enough: the crazy
Eyes, the hand held high taking his bloody vow. The very image of

The Prophet. And yet what did he prophesy? Ask the ghosts at
Potawatomi. Ask Bleeding Kansas. Ask *him* for that matter.
He failed at everything he did including his famous stand at Harpers Ferry,
And America builds him a boulder, encloses his tombstone in dingy glass,
And pays a guard to live there in the shadow of the Mountain,
Just to sit by a window, waiting for someone to show.

This is the same nation that denied Pollock a cigarette. I don't know anything.
In spite of all I pray today, for myself, for *the Republic for which he stood.*
I leave here puzzled, a couple of brochures thrown into the backseat,
Mosquito bitten, sunburnt. Still, that white-faced mountain is a mystical sight.
One night two boys slipped out. They spent the night on its cold slope.
As far as I know it was their one free night. They are buried here too.

DIVA

We sought a finer sound that could lift up
Bathetic faces from their drowsy tiers,
A voice to reconstruct the standard plot
Into an altar high and lit in the figured air.

(It was, of course, the air we loved, the air
Tilting half-way between the universe
And our snug shod feet, tense as though to spring.)
We found it in the echoes of a life

Lived somewhere else than ours. A heroine
We'd overlooked. A tragedy made supple
By air reborn into our own mad scenes.
We couldn't help but hear, in her tortured breath,

As Violetta dying separates
The syllables of joy, that what we'd lost
Was well worth losing. And the house,
Gone dark after the last punishing blows,

Was silent for—what?—a moment?
We listened as we listen now: to nothing—
The voice we sought was nothing in the air.
She died of singing and of silence. Now,

Her coffin passes by to wild applause,
That still can cry out what we cannot sing:
We are an ugly race, abandoned, glorious.
We take this more seriously than we can say.

THE BROKEN GULL

First, disregard the shattered plume, the edge
Of fence unwinding where the carcass lies,
The feathers darkly plastered, stiff, at odd,
Unpleasant angles splaying from the bones.
Ignore all but the pearly eye transfixed
In blank perception of the unfurled flame.

It is as if some other world, aflame
With useless muscle touches us, edge on edge,
And, purple-gray, its signature has fixed
Itself upon this beach where we wanted to lie
And feel the sunlight loosening our bones
Into the texture of sand. It seems odd,

We never plan to be undone by odds
So entirely weighed against us, as if flame
Could not burn, and marrow in the bones
Not gradually thin till, standing on an edge,
Hollow and squinting, we see the cards that lie
Face up, and realize the game was fixed.

Or when a landscape seems fixed
So that the intrusion of some odd
Detail washing ashore to lie
In front of us is like a house in flames
On an otherwise peaceful block, we age
A little in the heart and in the bones.

And what seemed, once, more than clattering bones,
A sense of ourselves in which the soul was fixed,
Fades visibly with some offhand remark, the edge
Of which can cut us to the core at odd,
Unpleasant angles; whatever tiny, tended flame
Aroused us to this beach has flickered; we lie

Somewhat further apart than how we'd lie
As children with children's springing bones,
Our minds unfluttered like a holy flame
On which we'd dote with wonder, fearless, transfixed,
Never completely perceiving our odd
And precarious perch: toes just over the edge.

Now, consider your own bones eaten by time's flame.
Think of them as odd the way they lie
At the edge of your life: not quite broken, not fixed.

TWO

OBSESSIVE

Mozart made me want to play
Piano, made it sound easy.
Like painting. And speaking out loud
In a theater. A hundred things.

And you see, I have done these things.
Because they were. Easy.
But nothing is easy.
I *have* done one thing.

Another. Then another. None of them easy.
And soon I turn butterfly,
Indigo tenor warming up with scales;

The lips of His breath make the tiniest
Kissing sounds, echoes in the cupola:
Wingbeats. Transformation. It isn't easy.

Some days, today for example, waking's
A struggle: skating sleep's watery turns,
Not ready to trade the dream,
Confused as it thins into light.

Is this the same funereal light,
The same dream-pigeons in their turns:
Devastating—roof to sill to roof to sill?
Eventually, one gives up the dream.

And thankfully. *It was only a dream.*
Folds it up and closes the drawer.
This isn't beginning again, awakening.

The pigeon starts when I exhale
The dream. Have I loved more than loving
You? Have I done anything harder?

LIMELIGHT

I am not what I am. I am radiant.
Tonight I hide what's human in a drug.
I can't see what I'll kiss. I'm groping for
An armor wrap, a stranger's slung embrace.
And if, in the dark, I cannot see his face,
He's this week's trifle, skinny would-be thug,
My version of *amo, amat, amor.*
Or bridge-and-tunnel guppy, golden flame,
Who's swimming 'round the bowl, not noticing
That every turn around his life's the same.
Continually and chemically amused
We float through crowds, identities confused,
Hovering above ourselves, what angels want:
Held down by who we sing, by whom we're sung.

MISMALOYA BAY (Mexico: 1977)

Mistakes have made me. I wished them through.
Still, whispers reach me from the streets below.
I do not listen. They carry me.
Friends, but not enough to last, have carried me.

And written in a scrupulous hand, my estate,
Like a glyphed eye on limestone cliffs
Describes what I am and could not be
Without them. I have ruined my life more than once.

Surely the sign at the highway's turn conceals
A mystery, but what good is it to stop and gawk
At what an angler left to rib the world?

Arriving where I began, *je doute donc je suis,*
I cup my hand for potable water;
The sky's bruised tit releases what it can.

SPEAKING IN TONGUES

1.

He ran in cotton rows at War and Kings,
Sat in an elbow of an oak and ruled
The baked expanse, his half-built town, or crawled
Inside the grass in summer's deepest field.
He rode each winter Wednesday to the church
And altar-boyed, imagining the springs
Where he first knew the water's secret touch,
Where he first felt his body's flame unfurled.
He broke his own heart daily as he grew
Into a man he never planned to be.
He lost the days in whirlwinds as he threw
Cash to the bar and called for clarity.
But when he spoke to you, he'd only stutter.
And when he dreamed of you, he dreamed of water.

2.

In Oklahoma, during your hermit streak,
Cleaved to a cabined precipice above
A yawning gap, you played the King of Love
To outdoor audiences twice a week.
Magnetic, all vibration, but thin and weak,
You seemed so ready for the dazzling dove
To enter you that when you saw me off,
I thought that if I spoke to you, you'd break.
Since then I see you everywhere, in crowds,
In libraries, the laundromat, the stage.
As Christ, in dreams you reach for me: both hands
Are cupped and spilling over at their edge
With white and weightless space to knit my words
Elastic, shocked, and struggling to the page.

3.

When we were here together, I admit
I must have seemed to you completely crazy.
And though that time is still a little hazy,
I do remember weeping quite a bit.
For my part you were like a glass of water:
Whenever I called or stumbled in, you smiled.
And while I overplayed the wicked child,
I'm glad you didn't have to watch me shatter.
Yet what was underneath those everyday,
Past-midnight calls and visits for a loan
Was what I never told you, what I fall
Away from telling now, sober and grown,
Because I still don't want to hear you say
That what I wanted wasn't possible.

4.

I'd like to take you home with me and keep
You like a pet to talk to, to compose
Sonnets and lullabies about, and sleep
With you. I want to wake and watch the rose
Light pine and swell inside of you. I want
You to think of me first when you wake up.
I want to climb into your belly and
Climb out. I want to run and never stop.
Who are you? Once, on New Year's Eve I thought
For ten long minutes you were here with me,
Walking down Mercer Street, up Broadway where
The drunken horns and floodlights shook the air.
It actually started snowing. Lover, lately
That night is all I ever think about.

MY FATHER'S SON

Today a northeast wind comes pushing down,
Tightens the cobbles, hardens the corn's dead flower,
A minute more of light for every hour.
      I wish I were a simpler man.

I watch his silhouette haloed with rain
Caught in streetlight scrim, still a shower
Between the dark and darker, but it's slower.
      His steps crescendo as he closes in.

He never looks. I never call him. He
Moves past me, but I run with what he's run,
      His complicated son.

In the end, he will lie underneath me,
His counsel quit, his daily waking done.
      I wish I were a quiet man.

BROKEN

Once I ran away into the night ten years
    There was no harm in the night any hand hot

At my belt at my shirt buttons I dreamed
    I sailed above them I was the deft man

So many years night boundless flexible
    Striped light through shudders the only hunger

Bracing the slim space between us I was
    Another there another wet city

Pond of yellow light swimming still blistered
    Wet roads hurricane the windows rattled

I was awake all night ten years away
    And sixteen since a quiet jungle

Once I ran away hard night slow night
    Whispers me still whispers still whispers

OUR LADY OF ABUNDANCE

No payoff at first. I swung my arms to dance,
Not sure how I should feel, if I should sing.
Late summer night. We *had* been studying.
He stood and as he moved, as though by chance,

He let his blue cloth robe drop to the floor.
His cock was only inches from my face.
I stared at him. Now, I don't remember
Any feeling. Timelessness? Even less.

The next time we smoked, it hit me. I avoided his hand.
Later I made him my first *particular* friend.
By then he had a girlfriend and a car.

The next year brought me booze and another, much
More passionate, confused, destructive. Such
A waste. *He* drove headfirst into his last closed door.

FOR BARBARA & VINCENT

1. Perhaps Our Woes are Inescapable

What matter that these maple branches decked
    With dapple-fall stand skewered in a tire
    Of styrofoam articulately packed
        Where, sooner than I want, a Christmas tree
Will twinkle artlessly into the night?

Just this: that I would trade the world's
    Inheritance for their gaudy, utterly blank,
    Unblemished pain. I would unswindle
        Every child and watch her grow. I would
Prevent her as a mournful light from every

Shame. Zosima was right. We *are* all
    Guilty. And on behalf of all, I cut
Three jeweled limbs of loveliness-in-death
    To decorate this corner of our life.

2. Home Movie

Four months colder than a hundred miles south,
    In rented rooms, a house George Washington slept in,
Built, or bypassed, we wasted an afternoon,
    Crowded near a fire, to watch *Hiroshima
Mon Amour* without a soundtrack. Brian
    Kept insisting the film was made that way.
I slipped away as often as I could
    To steal a shot, straight from the bottle,
Someone's Christmas gift. I didn't ask
    Permission. Easier to beg forgiveness if you're caught.
I thought whiskey would make the day more real.
    But, twenty years later, sober fifteen,
I'm still afraid of hearing what I missed.

3. Insomnia

Night's fist of darkness loosens as the sun
  Gives me another puzzle how to sing.
    It's 7:30 and I haven't slept
At all this night. Or any night for days.

Virgil wrote Eclogues. I need another form
  That tells about the sunrise on our towers,
    Its daily alchemy. Pedestrians
Do not, as a rule, look up, and so they miss

    Epiphanies: at my window, our family of falcons
  Secure in their Fifth Avenue zip code,
Out for a morning soar, hungry angels
    Caught in a snapshot. None will see
  As I have seen: hawk shadows on the gold
As momentary as the light itself.

AGAINST STEVENS

Truth is I have not sentiments for sleep.
The common tongue, the way you say we are
In *your* concupiscence, I thought I had to keep
The hill in Tennessee stoic, mystic its jar.
You've bullied me too long for me to call
You uncle, hero, St. Wallace of Hartford.
It may take years to clear my ear of all
The Evenings Without Angels I have heard.
But give self second thoughts, my doctor said,
When speech is at its zenith stay inside.
I take her advice quite seriously, she is
A true diva in my book. So let this ride
Its cycle for a while, but not your head
That makes me whole, your words me wise.

I dreamed of Schiller's head cascading down
The capitol; that he proposed this in a song.
Surrounded by human cattle deceived by slogans,
They took his word of universal bond
And sacrifice as one. But it was only warning,
A song for female voice. This is its text.

We are all republicans. Prevent us
O Lord in all our doings, etc.

I lost my love and turned to brotherhood;
What difference does it make? The sun supplies
The songs their hydrogen, the texts their freeze,
And all is dissipated in the general thaw.
The epigrams themselves, exposed, are bridged,
And every word is lit to show its teeth.

NIETZSCHE AT BAYREUTH: 1876

The summer closes with a cosmic fit,
But seasons avoid me. Here, I don't exist.
Some doze off, grimly vested, dimly lit
By crackling gowns: these husbands on a list:
Official Friends. Who understands these men?
Why did they choose this myth, this four-day show
To nap beside their wives. It's far too slow
A penance for their sorrow and their spite.

I fool myself that all of us are one
Standing beneath the final D-flat shine
That overflows the rafters and the Rhine.
But all of us are guilty, and the stains
Rinse equal in the artificial sun
From these hard chairs above the world's remains.

DAS LIED VON DER ERDE

From nowhere caught, the song
Carves me the way I suppose
Some fabulous distinction carves—a love
Returned, a death, or sound itself whose dreams
Grow solid in their lying down, whose layers
Fix, like fins, their depths
And render them maneuverable.

                                   I cannot
Move while she is singing this. Why do we love
What crushes us?

                  Over distance, over trouble,
The shadowed marshes bend against themselves,
Bend to a borrowed wind, in time, unmeasured.
The moon forgets to rise on the Yellow River.
A sad man mourns dead lovers in his sleep
With no one left. Forever. No one left.

BRINDISI

Can't sing a drinking song today and so
Can't tell his secret prayers on borrowed beads.
Can't line his empties up in rows as though
A saint his sins, a hunter his stuffed heads.

Can't lie in darkness weeping for the light.
Can't turn his friends to surrogates for his
Fanatic passions as no one in sight
Seems worth the trouble to seduce or please.

But, scourged and bound by how he's learned to see,
As in the shine from smoke-scarved rivers: pain,
He sweats the bloody sweat of poetry,

And writes the poison out but not the stain,
So that his vocal chords, wanting to burst,
Can only sing today with Christ: I thirst.

Baled in grave gray, this photo is three-quarters
Triangle of enormous hair. I believe you when you say you
Are Beautiful, Generous, Untimely. I believe your
Litter of Events. You are not their tree.
The Little Flower, enclosed in habit lived utterly free
And died a silent girl. You've not had freedom for one hour.
In the *Goldberg Variations* a pedestrian tune's
A rich man's lullaby made new:

We are neither bitch divas nor virgin martyrs.
We are these variations warmed with vigor of an obsolete
Triangle: composer, interpreter, listener, each with a job to do.
The theme is entrusted to you (whoever *you* are) as though
To raise it in your left hand, winsome, white,
And splinter the world, ordinary, slow.

CHRONIC

It seemed bed saws' grinding teeth; something churning
   in the sheets, carbide winter ahead, broiling sea at each equator
      where men's bones are oboes now, men like myself who have no name or too

many to fit one stone. Or simply no one. It was my
   room just off the hall. It was my
      vantage point: I watched my parents tear each other up.

        Light

brazen, invading my dark. It seemed that if I slept someone would go and
   not come back. He did and I was right to be alone. I've loved. But loved alone.
      And what does it matter now, thirty years late? Snapdragons, goldenrod,

tall tulips opening, autumned limbs arranged with pumpkin kids, gesture paintings,
   too many clothes, too many books; but just the right kaleidoscope. And then,
      there's always someone else to consider, his brain, his

      bearing.

BLESSING

He talked himself up woke to his own voice
    Full sentences questions strangled into

Speech now it feels like dawn raking wisp-thin
    Glory in his thrushed tongue he tries to say

To this day's noisy birds its rattled locks
    The words his dream spoke to the real morning

That it would congeal to hold him one breath
    He is to be here this day becoming

Shoulders hung with invisible harness
    Head-wanting-no-thing he mouths the dream grid

Only scaffolding now only the frame
    A rubbery bluster a new balloon

Of blood let go now let me into you
    Let day stay behind its blind slat shadows

FIRST MORNING LIGHT

1. Heroin

Through all the rain that year, summer was
Out-classed. Not a whisper about global warming.
Tight-chested, we defied the misty city
And almost lasted. August took my breath away.
Now what? Today I thought if God would offer me
A good disease, a month, painkillers, autumn,
A final exhalation, all the hymns
Chosen, the epitaph graven without flourish on
A simple, slender stone, white Carrera marble,
I'd take Him up on it. I wanted to cop today
On Avenue D. Instead, I met a man who needed me.
His name was James. I gave him ten dollars.
I told him I could respect someone who had
Fallen to the ground to see, who loved the bass notes.

2. Puerto Vallarta

Anger is the world's first poem's first word,
The rage of someone's son who's been shortchanged.
Sulking on my own, the room too hot,
I nurse my tit of rum till I'm content.
I hold the sunset in my hand and squeeze:
The night escapes from underneath my hat.
An old song from a city never built
Surprises this dusty land where they pray to the dead
For Vengeance, Liberty, the Tourist Trade.
Tonight, after closing the Piano Bar, Luis
Drives me out to the Pink Cantina no white man knows.
Scattered with human flamingos, the middle of nowhere
He shows me how to breathe beneath the glaze.
I hold him like a life-raft all night long.

3. Richard Smith (1944-1996)

The sky should have been metal-forged, pounded
Like Job's, a righteous man, with warning—of what?
But even then, who could have known that storms
Would be the least of grief? Furious summer.
I lost somewhere the will to flower then.
Console me. It will help. Everyone has an opinion.
I passed along the river to his wake.
The train stopped long enough to meet the rain.
No son or wife could understand the reason;
No girl imagined yet that he was gone.
An upright man, his family robbed, and given
The drifting rain, the puzzle of going on.
I thought there must be going on. I touched
His powdered hands and prayed he was not there.

4. Augustus Papaceno (b. 24 May 1996)

Impulse to breathe, heaving the torso through
The icy grip of someone else's world,
Bursting the crisp, sun-dazzled layer of the new
Stunned flesh you are: Augustus Papaceno.
How many thousand times you'll break our hearts,
To translate this into the you we'll know
(As we've done too, until that day this starts
Again, when from new wombs we're thrust, uncurled
And screaming at the air's first hardening).
I'll tell you a secret, boy: there is no other
Life. Your father's a gentle man. Your mother
Will love you like the sunrise loves the spring.
Risk love. It's worth the grief and bother.
And be relaxed—but ready for anything.

AN EXERCISE FOR LOVERS

Think of one of those afternoons before
A spring storm breaks. Think of the highway,
Quiet under the clouds as though it wore
Their bruised shadows like a scarf, a gray
Canopy of bloom, steel on silver,
Until the curtain tears, the wind shakes
And seems to drop, injured, a white blister
Rips beyond the city to Seven Lakes
Where we saw the wild swan. We sat on the slate,
Chilled, shivering. Think of those lakes
From the city. Think of the lightning there.
I almost kissed you. But that larger weight
On the water seemed a warning: the mirror breaks.
Think of the swan as though it didn't care.

WHAT TO DO WHAT TO SAY

Don't look at a mirror for several days.
Reform the hollow just above the tongue
Below the roof till its occlusion says
What it will name you then. Inside the lung,
A breath lies waiting to surround the word
That breathed before you, beating in the ground.
Sometimes at night it climbs out like a bird
And looks at you, and folds its wings around
Your rising, falling frame. It licks your ears
And whispers *I've come home. I'm home for you.*
That shadow stretched out on the hill is mine.
Begin to speak as though you would to one
You've never seen but heard about for years.
Say this: It was all true. It was all true.

THREE

CREATION (Rodin)

Raise this, maestro: tons of ice, truckloads scraping below my window.
  Whole bins of hard snow grinding toward the River. I pray
    For tight leaves sleeping,
      Lime-pale, translucent, not even leaves, ideas of leaves.
Thawed sap stirring; first blood of spring flashing from a New Year's penny,

Raise this *miglior Fabbro*, in your spheric hand: our neighborhood's
  Bum muttering sidewalk conspiracies, roaring the
    Internationale,
      Slept through the blizzard. I thought he must be underneath.
But there he is today, Castro and Congo, paper cup trembling.

I'll bet the boy who runs the video store showed him the subway.
    Can't buy him a sandwich. Container of coffee? Sure.
      Something stronger? Sure.
    No forbidden fruits, not even a doughnut? No teeth.
You know Lord how we hate to be patronized. *Just a cigarette.*

Don't wait till the Last Day. Remember Cuba, and Gettysburg and
  The visions of all holy fools. The video boy.
      What a wondrous face
    Too. I imagine your face like that, all business,
But that beautiful. He took offense. It was only a thank you.

He didn't need it from me. The woman who sleeps near Calvary,
  The thrift shop man's Caribbean vowels, copper, sunburnt,
      (*Imagine: sunburnt!*)
    Help her back to us. Does she know her name? No matter.
We are all of us raised toward evening, toward the giant snow.

We watch the moon's sickle, lazy eyelid, dimmed by the Opera,
  By streetlights, cars. We adorn ourselves, give your light back.
      We hang, your pendant,
    Blue globe, steaming amulet, Paradise of Desire
Lifted to the oyster light, your jewel at night's deep-shadowed throat.

ICI (Joan Mitchell)

The plane is on the floor.
The plane is empty, numberless.
The plane has teeth. It is

Here, a longing with walls,
Accessory before the fact,
Revealer, destination.

The woman above the plane is
Irrelevant. She is
Empty, numberless,

A tunnel of revelation.
What will she do? Between
The woman and the plane is

Void and Without Form. It
Hovers for something to happen.
Something happens.

APOLOGY (Willem de Kooning)

I like painting big women
I am secure painting large women most men
Will not say this power will not name this girth
Men want each other Earth
Is a big woman sunrise
A big woman on the sea
Flaunting revealing embracing me
I wish you would sit for me my fortissima my prize

The man breathes as he paints her she is truth
Light catches her a memory of birth
Strikes off the sea knits the composition
Her bosom is full this is not a problem
If he could say what he feels he might call it youth
Held up by light held down by earth

GRAY AND GREEN (Mark Rothko)

Out of nowhere into nowhere nothing spreads,
Or lies, or floats, intensest at no point
Particular but this, divided by
Tall screens and carved and housed
For wandering outside the rectangle

To what its walls cannot enclose.
Or how the mind can go entirely dark
So that the hand can see, so that the dark
Can breathe, so that the light can never hide,
Being swallowed up, being rescued.

One wants a candle to the gray, the green,
A slender flame elegant as an elbow,
Or smoke to lift its call, or only air,
Or only knowledge that is knowledge of
Nothing that is here,

Pearl of great price, and small, and still,
And always wakeful, watching for the night.
The man whose crooked fingers saw the light
And hid it here, and covered it, and bled
Himself completely out, not rescued, not

Appraised, over and over, and larger still,
And here, the brightest number of his sight
Is zero housed in black and white
A room without him, always without him,
Always away.

AUTUMN RHYTHM

I deny the accident. . . . The result is the thing.

Jackson Pollock

I found you everywhere where I was not
        haze of stars   jazz bramble
    buried lakes
    a perfect undistinguished thing
        the accident
    slain at the foundation of the world

I called you from antiquity
                  sacrifice
the great whales surfaced to horn the air's first music

    you woke in their waiting
    each thing assembled
    there was not one missing

I honed you in the frigid shack
    stained and reeling   humid flame
    till the glad dance rained   the lung erupted
    each riff a rose in a lasso of black

I traced your lattices and violet heights
    the dark claimed the water
    the dark claimed the light

you are the word I could not say
        the syncopated stop
    the halt
           the outstretched arm
    it is autumn now

    dark as a penny
    as woodsmoke
    paper leaves
    as now in the crisp wind

    I vanish entirely
a boulder of absence in the tangled air

PIETA (Michelangelo)

At first it may not seem so, but the form
Inflates. And in particular, her hands:
The one we see that's opening extends
Above the knee; the other, under his arm,

Supports the lifeless mass where once he dwelt
Among us. He is surprisingly small
On her enormous lap, as though when all
That burden drained into the world, he knelt

And crumpled there, a rag, a broken wing.
And she, because she understands, because
She understood that spilling out and was,
From the beginning, opened, opening,

Receives and swells, becomes again the ark
Of all that light and pain. She does not weep.
She stares at him as though he were asleep
And bares him like a lamp against the dark.

ANNUNCIATION (Fra Angelico, Cell 3, Convent of San Marco, Florence)

She watches the attitudes of water
>the hunter's dive
>the eye of the prey in burdened dark

she waits for the eye to comprehend
>but comprehension does not come until
>that moment when the sky
>abruptly shows the water's trick

the motors move that move all motors here
>necessity's a broken limb still green in the rain
>its cry was never heard until she turned

to watch the water and the water's glare
>a tear in space where light and dark commune
>a personal place for which there is no word
>because no one would notice so caught up

strangely she notices strangely
>she is not surprised
>that light and water speak to her and say

>*you might have come here at any time*
>>*there is no time*
>>>*you sit at the edge of earth*
>>>*to see the moment sparked by nothing more*
>>*than the insisting thrust of every moment's birth*

>*how can the child have learned the crime*
>>*but by believing the silent ghost behind the door*
>>>*a rush of wind in the dark*
>>*a moment's hard release of stifled breath*
>*a casualty this is the begging hour*

>*warmed with flat supernal light*
>>*you can see sound you can walk around it*
>>>*you cannot keep it however the rains will come*
>>*the soft rain in the desert counting time*
>*whispering news of great joy*

she sees all this and hears it in herself
      the word and water and the girl
      reflected ghostly on the ebb and swirl

who only knows the words for yes and yes
      she is the prey and bird the shelf
      between the water and the wind
      the crossing road of every moment's try

to turn itself into no other thing
      within her large embrace than fullness
      the bell whose tone the river's noise obscures

and when she looks up
      it is another world her having heard
      a word in the water
      and in the fire over the water

a name in the mouth's occlusion
      spoken without sound
      the sycamores lean over her in lazy awe

she has something important to do
      she will go to her cousin in the far hill
      amazing
      she will tell her everything

LATE READING

In a novel I'm reading some guy name Marvin wins
The Yale with a slim volume: *The Delights of Death.*
    It's supposed to be
    A wink to the reader
I think. I take it personally, however,
From an otherwise satisfying read.

As though the Yale is available to the
Naiveté, irrelevance, self-
    Importance of youth.
    As though under forty
Is youth. As though poetry, as we're tirelessly told,
Makes nothing happen. (Or makes Nothing *happen.*)

Already a corpse, you wait for me on a beach
Double-darkened. Night smothers the deeper shelf of sea
    Moving and motionless.
    The tarp that covers you
Weighted randomly by blown sand, barely swayed
By the scraping of stiff wind, hardly

Rises from the dunes, hardly shows at all the knolls
Of a body once lithe, once clumsy and treasured,
    Once a living man.
    I'm somewhere else, being
Scolded I think, being fired, discovered,
My con exposed. Even close friends are hostile.

In the book of my mind, on a single page where the sea
With visible intensity moves undeterred
    Inevitably
    To claim you, I listen
As wind gasps in the folds of your body,
Sings to me in a strange language. But I am

Distracted by betrayals, by sharp explosions
Of anger: I have no idea, they are saying,
    How lazy I am,
    How frustrating it is
To love me. My sums don't add up. *Adios*
Says the pay-stub. Take your money and go. Now.

In the novel the delights of death signal to
The protagonist but remain alien. They are
    Still urgent, still bright
    As the face in his face,
The Younger Poet who (we sigh) finally smiles.
But it might as well be in tongues. Exit the hero.

He will not understand this. *And he must.* Thus,
The dénouement: a hand on his shoulder. A dream
    Forgotten as soon
    As the effulgent light
Demands, like the lapping sea, his attention, come
To carry off his mystery, his pearl of great price.

In another dream, I approach you. You are not
Buried in this one, not rotting or turning to salt.
    You are clean, white shirt,
    Grinning, glorified. You
Take my hand as we glide into a burnished pew.
And then we are singing. Together. A congregation.

WHERE I WOULD NOT GO

What I haven't learned from movies my father
Whispers to me in code the long nights
Sleep will not come. I have forgotten how to believe

In Safe Passage; consequently I have been listening
To my father a good deal lately. He says
I'm home for you and half the time I know

He's lying but some nights all it takes
Is one good word: you say my name
For example; I hear it and distinctly know

We are all loved and spoken for and nothing else matters.
Clocks subtract with or without hands, wine tastes
Like gasoline and I stare down my eyelids

Till shadows thin, tomorrow drops into its slot,
A perfect fit, and I must have slept sometime,
How else could I dream you.

In winter this occurs less often, but when it is
Spring, when invisible revolvers
In the slim trunks of Crape Myrtle cock,

Release, and slow-motion, suddenly,
The low music of a million bees
And all the fields are white,

I am standing in the middle of myself;
I am a goddamn little boy again
And cannot lose the furrowed look

Of someone waiting for a man in his car to burst
Shouldering the hill. And you are there, silhouette
Of no one exactly, of no body but mine.

MY BROTHER'S GHOST

Here where I labor
    The last light widens
        Soft as a rim of footprints,
        A thumb of blood flattening,
    Fading stain, slow-motion, in the arithmetic
        Of rivers.

Below me a ruined man shivers
    Tracking the swing of his shadow.
        Lines break from limbs in every direction;
        The last five leaves hang tight to the horizon
    Still believing that the drowsy syrup means
        Life everlasting.

After so many windows,
    Long since the light thinned fluttering,
        I left him behind me,
        Fogged breath in the hollow of stairways,
    A lingering straightness of blue above
        The beautiful river.

And here where I labor, where I had not hoped,
    He finds me: an explosion of pigeons,
        A stutter of wind in trees on the water,
        A perfect crowd of clouds mirrored
    In whisky colored glass, the only heaven there is
        Not imagined, not far.

JUST BY DECIDING IT

If you were with me, I'd be thinking
Of a drive out to the white lake
Even though it's raining.
We could watch the mallards' mating dance
And eat a hamburger, or listen
To Vivaldi on the radio, an oboe and guitar.

Once I tried learning to play the guitar.
You're always thinking
I know how, but I don't. If you'd listen
When I tell you these things . . . The lake
Is rattled now, I imagine, by the dance
Of lightning, flocks ascending. The reigning

Species this fall is blue teal, but when it's raining
They disappear. Sometimes I've picked up your guitar
As if, just by deciding it, my fingers could dance
Over the strings. And I wouldn't be thinking
About anything but, maybe, mist on a lake,
And I'd step out of my body and listen.

Brent, listen:
You can hardly hear it raining
From the banks that surround our tender lake
Like the body of a guitar
Around its vacant well. Thinking
About it, not like a death, but like a dance,

We are locked arm in arm; the dance
Depends on the distance between us. We listen
For the counterpoint, thinking
It's our one hope: to love rain when it's raining.
The flood hits the roof like chords on a guitar.
If we were together the lake

Could be all ours. No one comes to the lake
On a day like this. No one watches ducks dance
Or holds his breath to hear their quiet—*Listen*—
Almost inaudible banter, like me on the guitar:
Strumming but muted. It has stopped raining.
If you were here, what would we be thinking?

I lie down by the lake and listen.
Stop thinking for a minute. It isn't even raining.
That's you in the ground dancing. That's me on the guitar.

JUST THE FACTS

Sex captured me suddenly at thirteen:
I woke to find my roommate in my mouth.
It was boarding school, I admit. But still,

Even as I struggled to oblige, there
Was nothing of pleasure, of morning light.
He never bothered me again or spoke

Of it. A series of chance encounters
(I remember names: Tommy, Ronald, Jeff)
Resembled the first. It's no great wonder

I turned somewhat shy, unavailable,
Though I couldn't have said so then. Instead,
I hid inside my body like a cave.

New York, 1979, was full
Of opportunity. I passed. What if
I hadn't haunts me now most every day.

Death began in '84 with Michael.
I took him to the doctor one cold day.
Persistent cough. Lesions. The usual.

He died two, three months later. *Dulce et
Decorum est.* Then Jack and Detlief. Now,
I close my eyes and cannot count them all.

Then, last September, Dean. Unkindest cut.
I lay all night listening to him cough.
Sometimes it wakes me. A dead man coughing.

What if the sky's own body were a corpse
Spread like a tent, infecting us with light?
I climbed out by last fall and met a man

Who gave himself to me and smiled and said,
"Whatever you want." *Whatever I want.*
Unfortunately, he didn't have it.

ALL ROADS LEAD TO KANSAS

That was his answer. It was his only
Explanation. He chose a place to die
Where life had chosen him. No longer home—
His elders dead, his brother distant, a

Stranger—now nowhere, no one's, he found his
Last room: a place from which to organize.
Details occupied him. Minutes. He did
What he could and left the rest to Kansas.

I saw him in August. He was whiter.
His skin had let go of its frame. His eyes
Had grown. He was lucid, translucent, proud.
He coughed all night a garbage bag of blood.

What is a bag of blood? What does it mean
To see such a thing? A white garbage bag,
Half-full, opaque, disguised as life.
What has a man left who has tendered this thing?

It is a thing of earth turned inside out.
The inside of a man. He can shore it,
Pollute the green fields that bore him; and still
It's all inside, it's all there killing him.

The morning I was there he emptied death
Into a patch of sunflowers. These are
Immune to the diseases of our hearts.
Sunflowers in August so huge you'd think

The whole world was redolent, green, summer.
He did this with love. As if emptying
A garbage bag of tainted blood
In a patch of Kansas was just one more

Detail, another legacy, a gift
To the soil that grew him, to the summer.
He should not have died there,
A still shimmering husk, nowhere, alone.

I have not lived one day unafraid.
And he was not afraid. I don't recall
Much that I said that trip. We slept a lot.
I don't remember leaving either. Well.

Eleven days later, my answering
Machine informed me of his gain. And of
The Kansas corn that's rich to have him home,
His business done, his business just begun.

ROSES

What men invented who invented the seasons
Was a body's map as bodies stretch and fall.
They set time's start at winter's edge to show

Coming is hard to an age and going out
Is coming all over. So it seems right
That I should love you and your body

My whole life. I cut roses when I was a boy
From my grandmother's yard. It was
Unclear to me then to leave them to their lives,

To their having opened overnight in spring.
Little boys amazed by flowers cried long cries
Anyway, to nights as clear as God's mind is silent.

But grandmothers take you as you come. What I know
Is that every day the roots of me are growing into you
Against all odds, that you are holding me in the earth.

Our bodies embark their seasons steady as weather.
Crosswinds meet on the ridges and crowd the air;
The sky is a glass of water. We are that good.

AT THE WEST STREET PIERS

Something about what matters
   Breathes in the twilight blushing
      Everything here on the piers.

Latin boys in tanktops
   Cycle by, winking and whistling.
      You ignore it. You smoke like a pro.

What I love most about
   This city is the light.
      Not only the natural light

Vesting each tenement
   With golden damask, unfolding
      Pumpkin dusks like gowns,

But also the light that salmons
   Busy hearts inside
      Our grown-up lives into children's.

A tourist takes our picture:
   Arms over shoulders like pals,
      Uninjured, unashamed.

In the shot, this crumbling pier
   Blinds like a Turner harbor,
      Light-infused and torched

From inside with *composition.*
   For a generous, frozen moment,
      There is no disease invading,

No shadow in this brief
   Caesura between day
      And the sure, descending night.

HEAVEN REASSIGNED

I was taught to make the Sign of the Cross
Anywhere near a Catholic church. God
    Lived there in a box.
     But I found myself,
Today, ready to bless myself passing
The Seagram Building in a cab. It's not

The first time either. Once, the Post Office
On Eighth, another time the Opera.
    I catch my hand half
    Raised, two digits curled
In reverence. But why? The city sends
So many blessings like fly balls—Catch them

And you'll know why you're here. I do, anyhow.
Last night I dreamed a poem called "Heather,"
    And though none of its
    Hammered strophes survived
Awakening, it's a sonnet, *each line
a Station of the Cross.* Imagine this:

Fields; Indian summer; field after field.
We are running fast, barely touching ground.
    Late light tips each blossom
    Waist-high, bloody.
We are young, boys in fact, flying through fields
Of heather. Now, look up: the city's arms

Embrace us—only Central Park, it's not
Some cave in Bethlehem, or drama set on
    A cloud-gilt hill. Lamps,
    Not the mind of God.
When we were little "Mind me" meant "Obey."
Thus, *mind* has its threats as well as rewards.

Now, its rather unnerving tendency
To hallow rings carillons of distrust.
    The world's reredos,
    Muscular skyscape,
Manhattan as window to—what—*telos?*
I had not thought to alter till today.

What I remember from the dream is this:
One breath of heather saved from a whole field,
    Proffered, a crisp page.
    The walls around us
Off-white: the room in Fra Angelico's
Annunciation, arches barely glyphed.

You bear it and smile: an Angel with news.
Good news, bad news, then, too good to be true.
    I thought it about
    Me. How typical.
I cannot hold you. I cannot be held.
What's left must suffice. And we never die.

WHAT COMES THROUGH HEARING

Afternoon spent listening to Bach's cello suites
Till the daze overtook us
And we went wandering the haunted streets
Miming the "last fulfillment of love,"
Indecent, but stately,
Leaving the bodies behind
As is so often, lately,
The case with us.
And something silver melted in the mind,
And something fluted free of my tongue,
Something both like and unlike words,
That gathered tightly and hovered above,
Quick, honeyed sounds like hummingbirds,
And cried their little cries,
And dusted my astonished eyes
With light not seen, but sung.

My dear, uncanny friend, it was then,
And only then (but what can I say?
I feel as though
The only one left who didn't know
Or notice something) I understood the face
That woke me, your red, red flower,
The sound of morning singing as it rose.
Because, for everybody there's an hour
Especially his own, a welcoming. God knows
We live for it, and after, we live away,
In music as it drifts through space,
Carved in the palm of the cellist's hand
As he finesses through the sarabande,
Which meant something else to someone long ago,
But to us—and I'm so grateful you are here—
That we are loved, if one by the other,
And someone's our father, someone our mother,
And there will be no pain or grief or fear
In our bodies floating down the beautiful river
For the next five minutes, and, perhaps, forever.

THE DEAD

They are so generous. They wait
Till the streets have gone quiet enough to sleep.
They show us around their new countries.
They show us what we wish for most

Is just there on a table. See how the slanted light
Opens the shadows of your outstretched arm?
The Cézanne pears that oddly decline to fall?
A bowl of peachcream roses? And where did *they* come from?

But with the dead explanations are beside the point.
Why not a bowl of roses, Miss Inez,
A cup of berry wine, a fresh white shirt? No polyester blends
In heaven. Just 501's, 7 oz. Cokes and breezy abundance.

Yesterday I saw how they carry you.
I stood on a sheer cliff, staring over:
A body covered with tarp on the broken shore,
And I knew it was you. The wind stuttered the tarp.

It was torn and green, held down by four stones.
Your hillocks trembled, your furrows stirred
Until you sank, and the sea was flat,
And no wave tore, and no wind rattled.

Once you were a rag doll in a bathtub of fire.
Once you called me long distance— Imagine!—You
Reversed the charges. *Si prega, questi posti
Sono riservati per i mutilati di guerra o lavoro.*

This on the *autobus* printed where you sat.
You lessened as it moved away. I watched
Your white hand waving, barely gripping
An invisible lightbulb, just like the Queen. Farewell, ghost.

I loved you while you lasted and I didn't even know, here
In the day's gravity. And I'm sure the reason you give me
Yourself in night cities and churches and houses burning
Is that you are and ever shall be. My mirror. My vocation.

ABOUT THE AUTHOR

STEPHEN MCLEOD GREW UP IN DALLAS, TEXAS AND HAS LIVED IN New York City since 1987. He was educated at Southern Methodist University, Columbia University, and the Fordham University School of Law. In 2000, his manuscript was one of four finalists for the Academy of American Poets' Walt Whitman Award, and one of seven finalists for Fordham University's Poetry Out Loud Award. Mr. McLeod currently lives in Brooklyn and works as an appellate attorney for the Brooklyn District Attorney.

THE MAY SWENSON
POETRY AWARD

THIS ANNUAL COMPETITION, NAMED FOR MAY SWENSON, HONORS her as one of America's most provocative, insouciant, and vital poets. In John Hollander's words, she was "one of our few unquestionably major poets." During her long career, May was loved and praised by writers from virtually every major school of poetry. She left a legacy of nearly fifty years of writing when she died in 1989.

May Swenson lived most of her adult life in New York City, the center of poetry writing and publishing in her day. But she is buried in Logan, Utah, her birthplace and hometown.